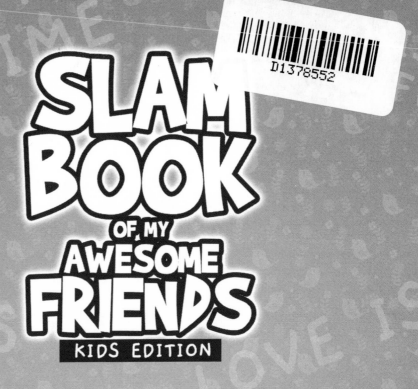

SLAM BOOK OF MY AWESOME FRIENDS

KIDS EDITION

THIS BELONGS TO:

ABOut mE

Name: ....

Nickname: ....

School: ....

STICK YOUR
BEST PHOTO
HERE!

fAVES

Hobbies:.......................................
....

Color:...

Snack:...

TV Series:.....................................

Movie:...

Book:..

Celebrity:.....................................

Band/Singer:...................................

Song:..

Role Model:....................................

Sport:...

Pet:...

Life Qoute:....................................
....

CIRCLE ONE

FACEBOOK or INSTAGRAM

SLEEP or PLAY

SING or DANCE

PIZZA or TACOS

SUMMER or WINTER

UNICORNS or PANDAS

MOUNTAIN or BEACH

MILK or CHOCOLATE

IPHONE or ANDROID

SWEET or SALTY

NIGHT or DAY

LOVE CORNER

Who is your BFF?

....

Who is your CRUSH?

....

Love is: ....

LEAVE A MESSAGE!

ABOUT ME

Name: ....

Nickname: ....

School: ....

STICK YOUR
BEST PHOTO
HERE!

FAVES ♥1

Hobbies:...
....

Color:...

Snack:..

TV Series:...

Movie:..

Book:..

Celebrity:...

Band/Singer:..

Song:..

Role Model:...

Sport:...

Pet:..

Life Qoute:..

....
....

CIRCLE ONE

FACEBOOK or INSTAGRAM

SLEEP or PLAY

SING or DANCE

PIZZA or TACOS

SUMMER or WINTER

UNICORNS or PANDAS

MOUNTAIN or BEACH

MILK or CHOCOLATE

IPHONE or ANDROID

SWEET or SALTY

NIGHT or DAY

LOVE CORNER

Who is your BFF?

....

Who is your CRUSH?

....

Love is: ....

LEAVE A MESSAGE!

ABOut mE

Name: ....

Nickname: ....

School: ....

STICK YOUR
BEST PHOTO
HERE!

fAVES

Hobbies:..
....

Color:..

Snack:..

TV Series:..

Movie:..

Book:..

Celebrity:..

Band/Singer:..

Song:..

Role Model:..

Sport:..

Pet:..

Life Qoute:..
....

CIRCLE ONE

FACEBOOK or INSTAGRAM

SLEEP or PLAY

SING or DANCE

PIZZA or TACOS

SUMMER or WINTER

UNICORNS or PANDAS

MOUNTAIN or BEACH

MILK or CHOCOLATE

IPHONE or ANDROID

SWEET or SALTY

NIGHT or DAY

LOVE CORNER

Who is your BFF?
....

Who is your CRUSH?
....

Love is: ....

LEAVE A MESSAGE!

ABOut mE

Name: ....

Nickname: ....

School: ....

STICK YOUR
BEST PHOTO
HERE!

fAVES ♥ 1

Hobbies:.......................................
....

Color:...

Snack:...

TV Series:.....................................

Movie:...

Book:..

Celebrity:.....................................

Band/Singer:...................................

Song:..

Role Model:....................................

Sport:...

Pet:...

Life Qoute:....................................
....
....

CIRCLE ONE

FACEBOOK or INSTAGRAM

SLEEP or PLAY

SING or DANCE

PIZZA or TACOS

SUMMER or WINTER

UNICORNS or PANDAS

MOUNTAIN or BEACH

MILK or CHOCOLATE

IPHONE or ANDROID

SWEET or SALTY

NIGHT or DAY

LOVE CORNER

Who is your BFF?

....

Who is your CRUSH?

....

Love is: ....

LEAVE A MESSAGE!

AbOut mE

Name: ....

Nickname: ....

School: ....

STICK YOUR BEST PHOTO HERE!

fAVES ♥ 7

Hobbies:...

....

Color:...

Snack:...

TV Series:...

Movie:...

Book:..

Celebrity:...

Band/Singer:...

Song:..

Role Model:..

Sport:...

Pet:...

Life Qoute:..

....

....

CIRCLE OlE

FACEBOOK or INSTAGRAM

SLEEP or PLAY

SING or DANCE

PIZZA or TACOS

SUMMER or WINTER

UNICORNS or PANDAS

MOUNTAIN or BEACH

MILK or CHOCOLATE

IPHONE or ANDROID

SWEET or SALTY

NIGHT or DAY

LOVE CORlER

Who is your BFF?

....

Who is your CRUSH?

....

Love is: ....

LEAVE A MESSAGE!

ABOut mE

Name: ....

Nickname: ....

School: ....

STICK YOUR BEST PHOTO HERE!

fAVES ♥1

Hobbies:....................................
....

Color:......................................

Snack:......................................

TV Series:..................................

Movie:......................................

Book:.......................................

Celebrity:..................................

Band/Singer:................................

Song:.......................................

Role Model:.................................

Sport:......................................

Pet:..

Life Qoute:.................................
....

CIRCLE ONE

FACEBOOK or INSTAGRAM

SLEEP or PLAY

SING or DANCE

PIZZA or TACOS

SUMMER or WINTER

UNICORNS or PANDAS

MOUNTAIN or BEACH

MILK or CHOCOLATE

IPHONE or ANDROID

SWEET or SALTY

NIGHT or DAY

LOVE CORNER

Who is your BFF?
....

Who is your CRUSH?
....

Love is: ....

LEAVE A MESSAGE!

ABOut mE

Name: ....

Nickname: ....

School: ....

STICK YOUR
BEST PHOTO
HERE!

fAVES

Hobbies:..
....

Color:..

Snack:...

TV Series:..

Movie:...

Book:...

Celebrity:...

Band/Singer:..

Song:...

Role Model:...

Sport:..

Pet:..

Life Qoute:...
....
....

CIRCLE ONE

FACEBOOK or INSTAGRAM

SLEEP or PLAY

SING or DANCE

PIZZA or TACOS

SUMMER or WINTER

UNICORNS or PANDAS

MOUNTAIN or BEACH

MILK or CHOCOLATE

IPHONE or ANDROID

SWEET or SALTY

NIGHT or DAY

LOVE CORNER

Who is your BFF?
....

Who is your CRUSH?
....

Love is: ....

LEAVE A MESSAGE!

ABOUT ME

Name: ....

Nickname: ....

School: ....

STICK YOUR
BEST PHOTO
HERE!

fAVES ♥1

Hobbies:...
....

Color:...

Snack:..

TV Series:..

Movie:...

Book:..

Celebrity:..

Band/Singer:..

Song:...

Role Model:..

Sport:..

Pet:..

Life Qoute:...
....
....

CIRCLE ONE

FACEBOOK or INSTAGRAM

SLEEP or PLAY

SING or DANCE

PIZZA or TACOS

SUMMER or WINTER

UNICORNS or PANDAS

MOUNTAIN or BEACH

MILK or CHOCOLATE

IPHONE or ANDROID

SWEET or SALTY

NIGHT or DAY

LOVE CORNER

Who is your BFF?
....

Who is your CRUSH?
....

Love is: ....

LEAVE A MESSAGE!

About me

Name: ....
Nickname: ....
School: ....

STICK YOUR
BEST PHOTO
HERE!

fAVES

Hobbies:...
....
Color:...
Snack:..
TV Series:...
Movie:..
Book:..
Celebrity:..
Band/Singer:...
Song:..
Role Model:...
Sport:...
Pet:...
Life Qoute:..
....
....

CIRCLE ONE

FACEBOOK or INSTAGRAM
SLEEP or PLAY
SING or DANCE
PIZZA or TACOS
SUMMER or WINTER
UNICORNS or PANDAS
MOUNTAIN or BEACH
MILK or CHOCOLATE
IPHONE or ANDROID
SWEET or SALTY
NIGHT or DAY

LOVE CORNER

Who is your BFF?
....
Who is your CRUSH?
....
Love is: ....

LEAVE A MESSAGE!

About Me

Name: ....

Nickname: ....

School: ....

STICK YOUR BEST PHOTO HERE!

fAVES ♥ 1

Hobbies:...
....

Color:..

Snack:...

TV Series:..

Movie:..

Book:..

Celebrity:...

Band/Singer:..

Song:...

Role Model:..

Sport:..

Pet:..

Life Qoute:...
....
....

CIRCLE ONE

FACEBOOK or INSTAGRAM

SLEEP or PLAY

SING or DANCE

PIZZA or TACOS

SUMMER or WINTER

UNICORNS or PANDAS

MOUNTAIN or BEACH

MILK or CHOCOLATE

IPHONE or ANDROID

SWEET or SALTY

NIGHT or DAY

LOVE CORNER

Who is your BFF?
....

Who is your CRUSH?
....

Love is: ....

LEAVE A MESSAGE!

ABOUT ME

Name: ....

Nickname: ....

School: ....

STICK YOUR
BEST PHOTO
HERE!

FAVES ♥ 1

Hobbies:...

....

Color:...

Snack:..

TV Series:..

Movie:..

Book:...

Celebrity:...

Band/Singer:..

Song:...

Role Model:..

Sport:..

Pet:..

Life Qoute:...

....

....

CIRCLE ONE

FACEBOOK or INSTAGRAM

SLEEP or PLAY

SING or DANCE

PIZZA or TACOS

SUMMER or WINTER

UNICORNS or PANDAS

MOUNTAIN or BEACH

MILK or CHOCOLATE

IPHONE or ANDROID

SWEET or SALTY

NIGHT or DAY

LOVE CORNER

Who is your BFF?

....

Who is your CRUSH?

....

Love is: ....

LEAVE A MESSAGE!

ABOut ME

Name: ....

Nickname: ....

School: ....

STICK YOUR
BEST PHOTO
HERE!

fAVES ♥1

Hobbies: ....
....

Color: ....

Snack: ....

TV Series: ....

Movie: ....

Book: ....

Celebrity: ....

Band/Singer: ....

Song: ....

Role Model: ....

Sport: ....

Pet: ....

Life Qoute: ....

....

....

CIRCLE ONE

FACEBOOK or INSTAGRAM

SLEEP or PLAY

SING or DANCE

PIZZA or TACOS

SUMMER or WINTER

UNICORNS or PANDAS

MOUNTAIN or BEACH

MILK or CHOCOLATE

IPHONE or ANDROID

SWEET or SALTY

NIGHT or DAY

LOVE CORNER

Who is your BFF?

....

Who is your CRUSH?

....

Love is: ....

LEAVE A MESSAGE!

ABOUT ME

Name: ....

Nickname: ....

School: ....

STICK YOUR
BEST PHOTO
HERE!

fAVES ♥1

Hobbies:..
....

Color:..

Snack:..

TV Series:..

Movie:..

Book:..

Celebrity:..

Band/Singer:..

Song:..

Role Model:..

Sport:..

Pet:..

Life Qoute:..
....
....

CIRCLE ONE

FACEBOOK or INSTAGRAM

SLEEP or PLAY

SING or DANCE

PIZZA or TACOS

SUMMER or WINTER

UNICORNS or PANDAS

MOUNTAIN or BEACH

MILK or CHOCOLATE

IPHONE or ANDROID

SWEET or SALTY

NIGHT or DAY

LOVE CORNER

Who is your BFF?
....

Who is your CRUSH?
....

Love is: ....

LEAVE A MESSAGE!

ABOUT ME

Name: ....

Nickname: ....

School: ....

STICK YOUR
BEST PHOTO
HERE!

FAVES ♥1

Hobbies:..
....

Color:..

Snack:..

TV Series:..

Movie:..

Book:...

Celebrity:..

Band/Singer:...

Song:...

Role Model:..

Sport:..

Pet:..

Life Qoute:..
....
....

CIRCLE ONE

FACEBOOK or INSTAGRAM

SLEEP or PLAY

SING or DANCE

PIZZA or TACOS

SUMMER or WINTER

UNICORNS or PANDAS

MOUNTAIN or BEACH

MILK or CHOCOLATE

IPHONE or ANDROID

SWEET or SALTY

NIGHT or DAY

LOVE CORNER

Who is your BFF?
....

Who is your CRUSH?
....

Love is: ....

LEAVE A MESSAGE!

ABOut mE

Name: ....

Nickname: ....

School: ....

STICK YOUR
BEST PHOTO
HERE!

fAVES ♥ 1

Hobbies: ....
....

Color: ....

Snack: ....

TV Series: ....

Movie: ....

Book: ....

Celebrity: ....

Band/Singer: ....

Song: ....

Role Model: ....

Sport: ....

Pet: ....

Life Qoute: ....
....

CIRCLE ONE

FACEBOOK or INSTAGRAM

SLEEP or PLAY

SING or DANCE

PIZZA or TACOS

SUMMER or WINTER

UNICORNS or PANDAS

MOUNTAIN or BEACH

MILK or CHOCOLATE

IPHONE or ANDROID

SWEET or SALTY

NIGHT or DAY

LOVE CORNER

Who is your BFF?
....

Who is your CRUSH?
....

Love is: ....

LEAVE A MESSAGE!

ABOUT ME

Name: ....
Nickname: ....
School: ....

fAVES ♥1

Hobbies:...
....
Color:..
Snack:...
TV Series:...
Movie:...
Book:...
Celebrity:..
Band/Singer:.......................................
Song:..
Role Model:...
Sport:..
Pet:...
Life Qoute:...
....
....

CIRCLE ONE

FACEBOOK or INSTAGRAM

SLEEP or PLAY

SING or DANCE

PIZZA or TACOS

SUMMER or WINTER

UNICORNS or PANDAS

MOUNTAIN or BEACH

MILK or CHOCOLATE

IPHONE or ANDROID

SWEET or SALTY

NIGHT or DAY

LOVE CORNER

Who is your BFF?
....
Who is your CRUSH?
....
Love is: ....

LEAVE A MESSAGE!

ABOUT ME

Name: ....

Nickname: ....

School: ....

fAVES ♥1

Hobbies:...
....

Color:...

Snack:..

TV Series:...

Movie:..

Book:..

Celebrity:...

Band/Singer:...

Song:..

Role Model:...

Sport:...

Pet:...

Life Qoute:..
....
....

CIRCLE ONE

FACEBOOK or INSTAGRAM

SLEEP or PLAY

SING or DANCE

PIZZA or TACOS

SUMMER or WINTER

UNICORNS or PANDAS

MOUNTAIN or BEACH

MILK or CHOCOLATE

IPHONE or ANDROID

SWEET or SALTY

NIGHT or DAY

LOVE CORNER

Who is your BFF?

....

Who is your CRUSH?

....

Love is: ....

LEAVE A MESSAGE!

ABOUT ME

Name: ....

Nickname: ....

School: ....

STICK YOUR BEST PHOTO HERE!

FAVES

Hobbies:...

....

Color:..

Snack:..

TV Series:..

Movie:..

Book:...

Celebrity:..

Band/Singer:..

Song:...

Role Model:...

Sport:..

Pet:..

Life Qoute:...

....

....

CIRCLE ONE

FACEBOOK or INSTAGRAM

SLEEP or PLAY

SING or DANCE

PIZZA or TACOS

SUMMER or WINTER

UNICORNS or PANDAS

MOUNTAIN or BEACH

MILK or CHOCOLATE

IPHONE or ANDROID

SWEET or SALTY

NIGHT or DAY

LOVE CORNER

Who is your BFF?

....

Who is your CRUSH?

....

Love is: ....

LEAVE A MESSAGE!

ABOUT ME

Name: ....

Nickname: ....

School: ....

STICK YOUR BEST PHOTO HERE!

fAVES

Hobbies:...
....

Color:..

Snack:...

TV Series:...

Movie:...

Book:..

Celebrity:...

Band/Singer:...

Song:..

Role Model:..

Sport:...

Pet:...

Life Qoute:...
....
....

CIRCLE ONE

FACEBOOK or INSTAGRAM

SLEEP or PLAY

SING or DANCE

PIZZA or TACOS

SUMMER or WINTER

UNICORNS or PANDAS

MOUNTAIN or BEACH

MILK or CHOCOLATE

IPHONE or ANDROID

SWEET or SALTY

NIGHT or DAY

LOVE CORNER

Who is your BFF?
....

Who is your CRUSH?
....

Love is: ....

LEAVE A MESSAGE!

ABOUT ME

Name: ....

Nickname: ....

School: ....

STICK YOUR
BEST PHOTO
HERE!

fAVES

Hobbies:..

....

Color:..

Snack:...

TV Series:.......................................

Movie:...

Book:...

Celebrity:..

Band/Singer:...................................

Song:...

Role Model:.....................................

Sport:..

Pet:..

Life Qoute:.....................................

....

....

CIRCLE ONE

FACEBOOK or INSTAGRAM

SLEEP or PLAY

SING or DANCE

PIZZA or TACOS

SUMMER or WINTER

UNICORNS or PANDAS

MOUNTAIN or BEACH

MILK or CHOCOLATE

IPHONE or ANDROID

SWEET or SALTY

NIGHT or DAY

LOVE CORNER

Who is your BFF?

....

Who is your CRUSH?

....

Love is: ....

LEAVE A MESSAGE!

ABOut ME

Name: ....
Nickname: ....
School: ....

STICK YOUR BEST PHOTO HERE!

fAVES ♥1

Hobbies: ....
....
Color: ....
Snack: ....
TV Series: ....
Movie: ....
Book: ....
Celebrity: ....
Band/Singer: ....
Song: ....
Role Model: ....
Sport: ....
Pet: ....
Life Qoute: ....
....
....

CIRCLE ONE

FACEBOOK or INSTAGRAM

SLEEP or PLAY

SING or DANCE

PIZZA or TACOS

SUMMER or WINTER

UNICORNS or PANDAS

MOUNTAIN or BEACH

MILK or CHOCOLATE

IPHONE or ANDROID

SWEET or SALTY

NIGHT or DAY

LOVE CORNER

Who is your BFF?
....
Who is your CRUSH?
....
Love is: ....

LEAVE A MESSAGE!

ABOut mE

Name: ....

Nickname: ....

School: ....

STICK YOUR
BEST PHOTO
HERE!

fAVES ♥1

Hobbies:...
....
Color:...
Snack:..
TV Series:..
Movie:..
Book:...
Celebrity:..
Band/Singer:....................................
Song:..
Role Model:.......................................
Sport:..
Pet:..
Life Qoute:..
....
....

CIRCLE ONE

FACEBOOK or INSTAGRAM

SLEEP or PLAY

SING or DANCE

PIZZA or TACOS

SUMMER or WINTER

UNICORNS or PANDAS

MOUNTAIN or BEACH

MILK or CHOCOLATE

IPHONE or ANDROID

SWEET or SALTY

NIGHT or DAY

LOVE CORNER

Who is your BFF?
....
Who is your CRUSH?
....
Love is: ....

LEAVE A MESSAGE!

ABOUT ME

Name: ....

Nickname: ....

School: ....

STICK YOUR BEST PHOTO HERE!

fAVES ♥ 1

Hobbies: ....
....

Color: ....

Snack: ....

TV Series: ....

Movie: ....

Book: ....

Celebrity: ....

Band/Singer: ....

Song: ....

Role Model: ....

Sport: ....

Pet: ....

Life Qoute: ....
....
....

CIRCLE ONE

FACEBOOK or INSTAGRAM

SLEEP or PLAY

SING or DANCE

PIZZA or TACOS

SUMMER or WINTER

UNICORNS or PANDAS

MOUNTAIN or BEACH

MILK or CHOCOLATE

IPHONE or ANDROID

SWEET or SALTY

NIGHT or DAY

LOVE CORNER

Who is your BFF?
....

Who is your CRUSH?
....

Love is: ....

LEAVE A MESSAGE!

ABOut mE

Name: ....

Nickname: ....

School: ....

STICK YOUR
BEST PHOTO
HERE!

fAVES ♥1

Hobbies: ....
....

Color: ....

Snack: ....

TV Series: ....

Movie: ....

Book: ....

Celebrity: ....

Band/Singer: ....

Song: ....

Role Model: ....

Sport: ....

Pet: ....

Life Qoute: ....
....
....

CIRCLE ONE

FACEBOOK or INSTAGRAM

SLEEP or PLAY

SING or DANCE

PIZZA or TACOS

SUMMER or WINTER

UNICORNS or PANDAS

MOUNTAIN or BEACH

MILK or CHOCOLATE

IPHONE or ANDROID

SWEET or SALTY

NIGHT or DAY

LOVE CORNER

Who is your BFF?
....

Who is your CRUSH?
....

Love is: ....

LEAVE A MESSAGE!

ABOut mE

Name: ....

Nickname: ....

School: ....

STICK YOUR
BEST PHOTO
HERE!

fAVES ♥1

Hobbies:..
....

Color:..

Snack:...

TV Series:..

Movie:..

Book:...

Celebrity:..

Band/Singer:...

Song:...

Role Model:...

Sport:..

Pet:..

Life Qoute:..

....

....

CIRCLE ONE

FACEBOOK or INSTAGRAM

SLEEP or PLAY

SING or DANCE

PIZZA or TACOS

SUMMER or WINTER

UNICORNS or PANDAS

MOUNTAIN or BEACH

MILK or CHOCOLATE

IPHONE or ANDROID

SWEET or SALTY

NIGHT or DAY

LOVE CORNER

Who is your BFF?

....

Who is your CRUSH?

....

Love is: ....

LEAVE A MESSAGE!

ABOUT ME

Name: ....

Nickname: ....

School: ....

STICK YOUR
BEST PHOTO
HERE!

fAVES ♥1

Hobbies:...

....

Color:...

Snack:...

TV Series:..

Movie:..

Book:..

Celebrity:..

Band/Singer:.......................................

Song:...

Role Model:..

Sport:..

Pet:...

Life Qoute:..

....

....

CIRCLE ONE

FACEBOOK or INSTAGRAM

SLEEP or PLAY

SING or DANCE

PIZZA or TACOS

SUMMER or WINTER

UNICORNS or PANDAS

MOUNTAIN or BEACH

MILK or CHOCOLATE

IPHONE or ANDROID

SWEET or SALTY

NIGHT or DAY

LOVE CORNER

Who is your BFF?

....

Who is your CRUSH?

....

Love is: ....

LEAVE A MESSAGE!

ABOUT ME

Name: ....

Nickname: ....

School: ....

STICK YOUR
BEST PHOTO
HERE!

fAVES ♥1

Hobbies:...
....

Color:..

Snack:...

TV Series:..

Movie:...

Book:...

Celebrity:...

Band/Singer:..

Song:...

Role Model:..

Sport:..

Pet:...

Life Qoute:...

....

....

CIRCLE ONE

FACEBOOK or INSTAGRAM

SLEEP or PLAY

SING or DANCE

PIZZA or TACOS

SUMMER or WINTER

UNICORNS or PANDAS

MOUNTAIN or BEACH

MILK or CHOCOLATE

IPHONE or ANDROID

SWEET or SALTY

NIGHT or DAY

LOVE CORNER

Who is your BFF?

....

Who is your CRUSH?

....

Love is: ....

LEAVE A MESSAGE!

ABOUT ME

Name: ....

Nickname: ....

School: ....

STICK YOUR
BEST PHOTO
HERE!

fAVES ♥1

Hobbies: ....

....

Color: ....

Snack: ....

TV Series: ....

Movie: ....

Book: ....

Celebrity: ....

Band/Singer: ....

Song: ....

Role Model: ....

Sport: ....

Pet: ....

Life Qoute: ....

....

....

CIRCLE ONE

FACEBOOK or INSTAGRAM

SLEEP or PLAY

SING or DANCE

PIZZA or TACOS

SUMMER or WINTER

UNICORNS or PANDAS

MOUNTAIN or BEACH

MILK or CHOCOLATE

IPHONE or ANDROID

SWEET or SALTY

NIGHT or DAY

LOVE CORNER

Who is your BFF?

....

Who is your CRUSH?

....

Love is: ....

LEAVE A MESSAGE!

ABOUT ME

Name: ....

Nickname: ....

School: ....

STICK YOUR BEST PHOTO HERE!

FAVES ♥7

Hobbies: ....
....

Color: ....

Snack: ....

TV Series: ....

Movie: ....

Book: ....

Celebrity: ....

Band/Singer: ....

Song: ....

Role Model: ....

Sport: ....

Pet: ....

Life Qoute: ....
....
....

CIRCLE ONE

FACEBOOK or INSTAGRAM

SLEEP or PLAY

SING or DANCE

PIZZA or TACOS

SUMMER or WINTER

UNICORNS or PANDAS

MOUNTAIN or BEACH

MILK or CHOCOLATE

IPHONE or ANDROID

SWEET or SALTY

NIGHT or DAY

LOVE CORNER

Who is your BFF?
....

Who is your CRUSH?
....

Love is: ....

LEAVE A MESSAGE!

ABOut mE

Name: ....

Nickname: ....

School: ....

STICK YOUR
BEST PHOTO
HERE!

fAVES

Hobbies: ....
....

Color: ....

Snack: ....

TV Series: ....

Movie: ....

Book: ....

Celebrity: ....

Band/Singer: ....

Song: ....

Role Model: ....

Sport: ....

Pet: ....

Life Qoute: ....
....
....

CIRCLE ONE

FACEBOOK or INSTAGRAM

SLEEP or PLAY

SING or DANCE

PIZZA or TACOS

SUMMER or WINTER

UNICORNS or PANDAS

MOUNTAIN or BEACH

MILK or CHOCOLATE

IPHONE or ANDROID

SWEET or SALTY

NIGHT or DAY

LOVE CORNER

Who is your BFF?
....

Who is your CRUSH?
....

Love is: ....

LEAVE A MESSAGE!

ABOUT ME

Name: ....

Nickname: ....

School: ....

STICK YOUR
BEST PHOTO
HERE!

FAVES ♥1

Hobbies:...

....

Color:..

Snack:..

TV Series:...

Movie:..

Book:..

Celebrity:...

Band/Singer:..

Song:..

Role Model:...

Sport:...

Pet:..

Life Qoute:..

....

....

CIRCLE ONE

FACEBOOK or INSTAGRAM

SLEEP or PLAY

SING or DANCE

PIZZA or TACOS

SUMMER or WINTER

UNICORNS or PANDAS

MOUNTAIN or BEACH

MILK or CHOCOLATE

IPHONE or ANDROID

SWEET or SALTY

NIGHT or DAY

LOVE CORNER

Who is your BFF?

....

Who is your CRUSH?

....

Love is: ....

LEAVE A MESSAGE!

ABOUT ME

Name: ....

Nickname: ....

School: ....

STICK YOUR BEST PHOTO HERE!

fAVES

Hobbies: ....

....

Color: ....

Snack: ....

TV Series: ....

Movie: ....

Book: ....

Celebrity: ....

Band/Singer: ....

Song: ....

Role Model: ....

Sport: ....

Pet: ....

Life Qoute: ....

....

....

CIRCLE ONE

FACEBOOK or INSTAGRAM

SLEEP or PLAY

SING or DANCE

PIZZA or TACOS

SUMMER or WINTER

UNICORNS or PANDAS

MOUNTAIN or BEACH

MILK or CHOCOLATE

IPHONE or ANDROID

SWEET or SALTY

NIGHT or DAY

LOVE CORNER

Who is your BFF?

....

Who is your CRUSH?

....

Love is: ....

LEAVE A MESSAGE!

ABOUT ME

Name: ....

Nickname: ....

School: ....

STICK YOUR BEST PHOTO HERE!

FAVES ♡1

Hobbies: ....
....

Color: ....

Snack: ....

TV Series: ....

Movie: ....

Book: ....

Celebrity: ....

Band/Singer: ....

Song: ....

Role Model: ....

Sport: ....

Pet: ....

Life Qoute: ....
....
....

CIRCLE ONE

FACEBOOK or INSTAGRAM

SLEEP or PLAY

SING or DANCE

PIZZA or TACOS

SUMMER or WINTER

UNICORNS or PANDAS

MOUNTAIN or BEACH

MILK or CHOCOLATE

IPHONE or ANDROID

SWEET or SALTY

NIGHT or DAY

LOVE CORNER

Who is your BFF?
....

Who is your CRUSH?
....

Love is: ....

LEAVE A MESSAGE!

ABOUT ME

Name: ....

Nickname: ....

School: ....

STICK YOUR
BEST PHOTO
HERE!

fAVES ♥1

Hobbies:..
....

Color:..

Snack:...

TV Series:...

Movie:...

Book:...

Celebrity:..

Band/Singer:.......................................

Song:..

Role Model:...

Sport:..

Pet:..

Life Qoute:...

....

....

CIRCLE ONE

FACEBOOK or INSTAGRAM

SLEEP or PLAY

SING or DANCE

PIZZA or TACOS

SUMMER or WINTER

UNICORNS or PANDAS

MOUNTAIN or BEACH

MILK or CHOCOLATE

IPHONE or ANDROID

SWEET or SALTY

NIGHT or DAY

LOVE CORNER

Who is your BFF?

....

Who is your CRUSH?

....

Love is: ....

LEAVE A MESSAGE!

ABOUT ME

Name: ....
Nickname: ....
School: ....

STICK YOUR BEST PHOTO HERE!

FAVES ♥1

Hobbies:...
....
Color:...
Snack:...
TV Series:..
Movie:...
Book:...
Celebrity:...
Band/Singer:..
Song:...
Role Model:..
Sport:..
Pet:...
Life Qoute:...
....
....

CIRCLE ONE

FACEBOOK or INSTAGRAM
SLEEP or PLAY
SING or DANCE
PIZZA or TACOS
SUMMER or WINTER
UNICORNS or PANDAS
MOUNTAIN or BEACH
MILK or CHOCOLATE
IPHONE or ANDROID
SWEET or SALTY
NIGHT or DAY

LOVE CORNER

Who is your BFF?
....
Who is your CRUSH?
....
Love is: ....

LEAVE A MESSAGE!

ABOut mE

Name: ....

Nickname: ....

School: ....

STICK YOUR
BEST PHOTO
HERE!

fAVES

Hobbies:..
....

Color:...

Snack:..

TV Series:.......................................

Movie:..

Book:...

Celebrity:..

Band/Singer:..................................

Song:..

Role Model:....................................

Sport:...

Pet:...

Life Qoute:.....................................
....
....

CIRCLE ONE

FACEBOOK or INSTAGRAM

SLEEP or PLAY

SING or DANCE

PIZZA or TACOS

SUMMER or WINTER

UNICORNS or PANDAS

MOUNTAIN or BEACH

MILK or CHOCOLATE

IPHONE or ANDROID

SWEET or SALTY

NIGHT or DAY

LOVE CORNER

Who is your BFF?

....

Who is your CRUSH?

....

Love is: ....

LEAVE A MESSAGE!

About Me

Name: ....

Nickname: ....

School: ....

STICK YOUR BEST PHOTO HERE!

fAVES ♥1

Hobbies: ....
....

Color: ....

Snack: ....

TV Series: ....

Movie: ....

Book: ....

Celebrity: ....

Band/Singer: ....

Song: ....

Role Model: ....

Sport: ....

Pet: ....

Life Qoute: ....
....
....

CIRCLE ONE

FACEBOOK or INSTAGRAM

SLEEP or PLAY

SING or DANCE

PIZZA or TACOS

SUMMER or WINTER

UNICORNS or PANDAS

MOUNTAIN or BEACH

MILK or CHOCOLATE

IPHONE or ANDROID

SWEET or SALTY

NIGHT or DAY

LOVE CORNER

Who is your BFF?

....

Who is your CRUSH?

....

Love is: ....

LEAVE A MESSAGE!

ABOUT ME

Name: ....

Nickname: ....

School: ....

STICK YOUR BEST PHOTO HERE!

FAVES

Hobbies:..

....

Color:...

Snack:...

TV Series:..

Movie:..

Book:..

Celebrity:...

Band/Singer:..

Song:..

Role Model:..

Sport:...

Pet:...

Life Qoute:...

....

....

CIRCLE ONE

FACEBOOK or INSTAGRAM

SLEEP or PLAY

SING or DANCE

PIZZA or TACOS

SUMMER or WINTER

UNICORNS or PANDAS

MOUNTAIN or BEACH

MILK or CHOCOLATE

IPHONE or ANDROID

SWEET or SALTY

NIGHT or DAY

LOVE CORNER

Who is your BFF?

....

Who is your CRUSH?

....

Love is: ....

LEAVE A MESSAGE!

ABOUT ME

Name: ....

Nickname: ....

School: ....

STICK YOUR
BEST PHOTO
HERE!

fAVES ♥1

Hobbies:...

....

Color:...

Snack:..

TV Series:..

Movie:..

Book:...

Celebrity:...

Band/Singer:..

Song:...

Role Model:..

Sport:..

Pet:...

Life Qoute:...

....

....

CIRCLE ONE

FACEBOOK or INSTAGRAM

SLEEP or PLAY

SING or DANCE

PIZZA or TACOS

SUMMER or WINTER

UNICORNS or PANDAS

MOUNTAIN or BEACH

MILK or CHOCOLATE

IPHONE or ANDROID

SWEET or SALTY

NIGHT or DAY

LOVE CORNER

Who is your BFF?

....

Who is your CRUSH?

....

Love is: ....

LEAVE A MESSAGE!

Made in the USA
Middletown, DE
25 June 2019